The bone

Series editor: Keith Gaines

Illustrated by Margaret de Souza

Nelson

"We are going for a picnic," said Rob.

"I will take the picnic food," said Rob's Dad.

"I will take the dog,"
said Rob.

"I will take the baby,"
said Rob's Mum.

They ate the picnic food.

"Here you are,"
said Rob's Mum.
"You can have the bone."

The dog took the bone.
He dug a hole.

He put the bone in the hole.
He filled up the hole.

"I will read my book," said Rob.

The dog took the toy cat.

He dug a hole.

He put the toy cat in the hole.

He filled up the hole.

"Look at the baby,"
said Rob.

"Give him his toy cat,"
said Rob's Mum.
"Can you see it, Rob?"

"No,"
said Rob.
"Can you see it, Dad?"

"No,"
said his Dad.
"But I think I can find it.

Did you take the toy cat?"
he said to the dog.

He dug up the toy cat.

"Here you are,"
he said.

He dug up the bone.

"Here you are,"
he said.
"You can't have the toy cat but you can have the bone."